WORD BUILDER

AGE 4+

LEVEL 1

ACTIVITY BOOK FOR CHILDREN

VOCABULARY MADE FUN

THIS BOOK BELONGS TO...

_ _

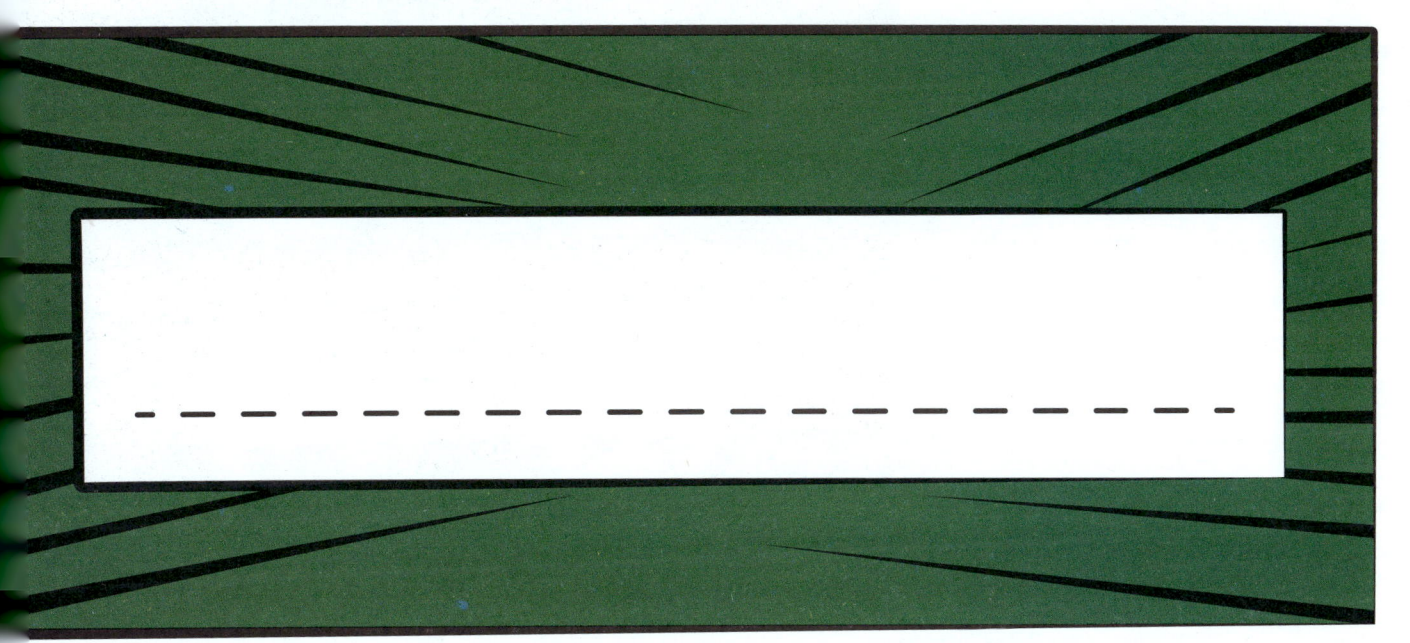

WORD BUILDER

CREATE WORDS WITH THE GIVEN SET OF LETTERS.

BONUS WORDS:

....
....
....
....

B T
A E

TIME TAKEN :

.... :

AT, TAB, EAT

2

WORD BUILDER

MAKE MEANINGFUL WORDS WITH THE GIVEN LETTERS.

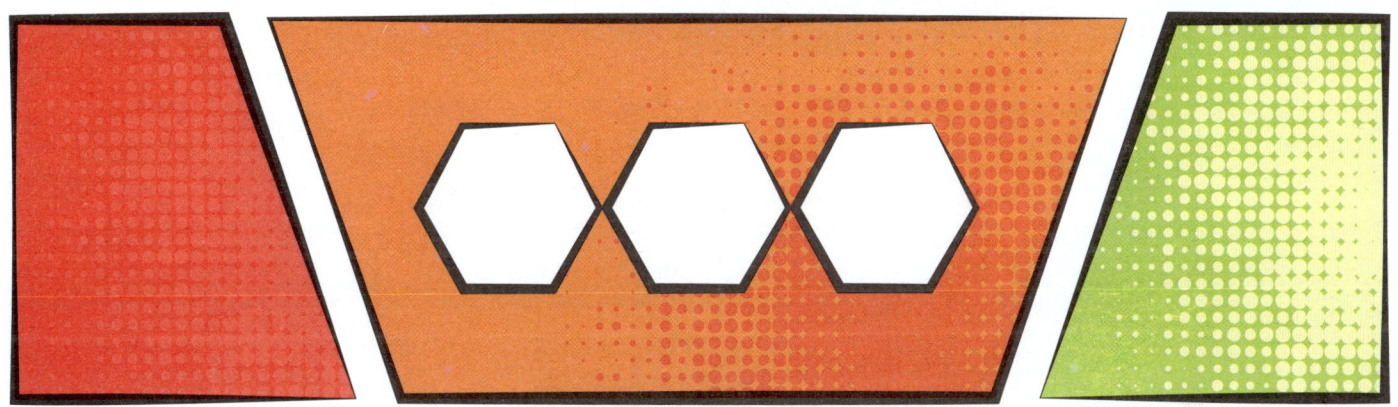

BONUS WORDS:

TIME TAKEN :

.... : ....

AS, APE, SAP

3

WORD BUILDER

MAKE AS MANY WORDS AS YOU CAN WITH THE GIVEN LETTERS.

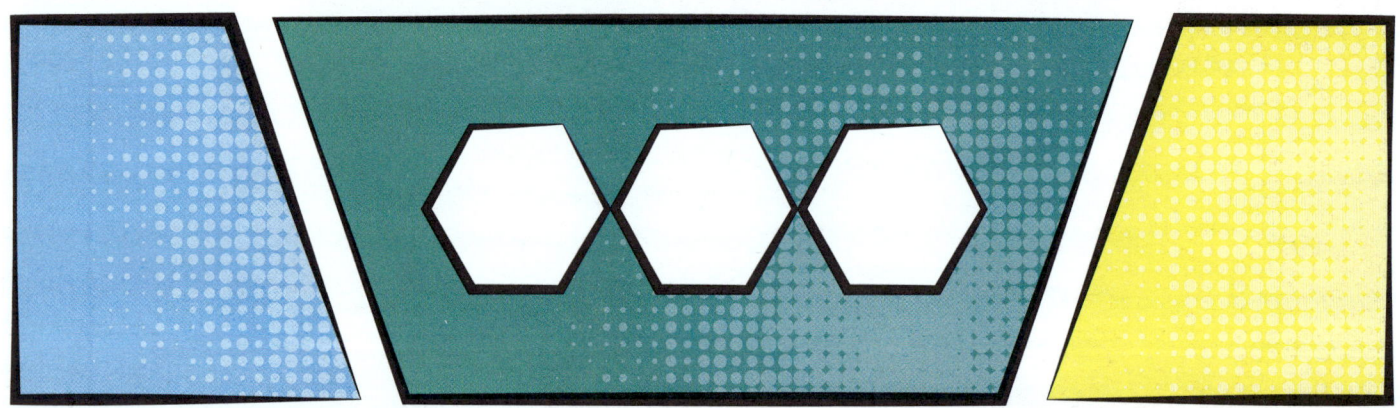

BONUS WORDS:

....

....

....

....

O F G R

OF, GO, FOG

TIME TAKEN :

:

....

4

WORD BUILDER

USE THE LETTERS TO FORM MEANINGFUL WORDS.

BONUS WORDS:

....

....

....

....

TIME TAKEN :

:

....

US, SUE, USE

5

WORD BUILDER

CREATE WORDS WITH THE GIVEN SET OF LETTERS.

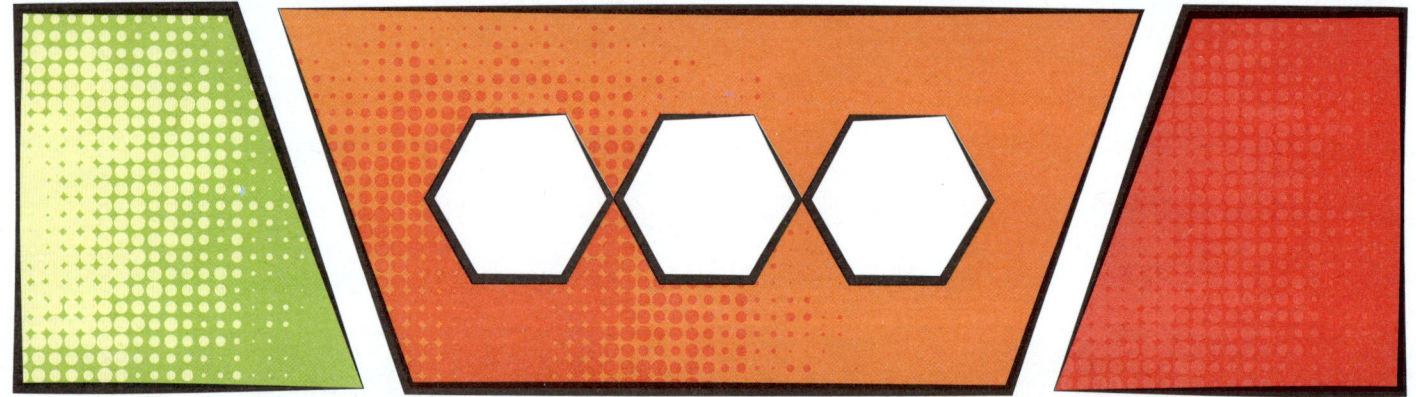

BONUS WORDS:

TIME TAKEN :

:

6

MAKE MEANINGFUL WORDS WITH THE GIVEN LETTERS.

BONUS WORDS:

TIME TAKEN :

US, BUS, SUB

WORD BUILDER

CREATE WORDS WITH THE GIVEN SET OF LETTERS.

BONUS WORDS:

AN, NAP, PAN

TIME TAKEN :

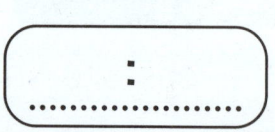

8

WORD BUILDER

MAKE MEANINGFUL WORDS WITH THE GIVEN LETTERS.

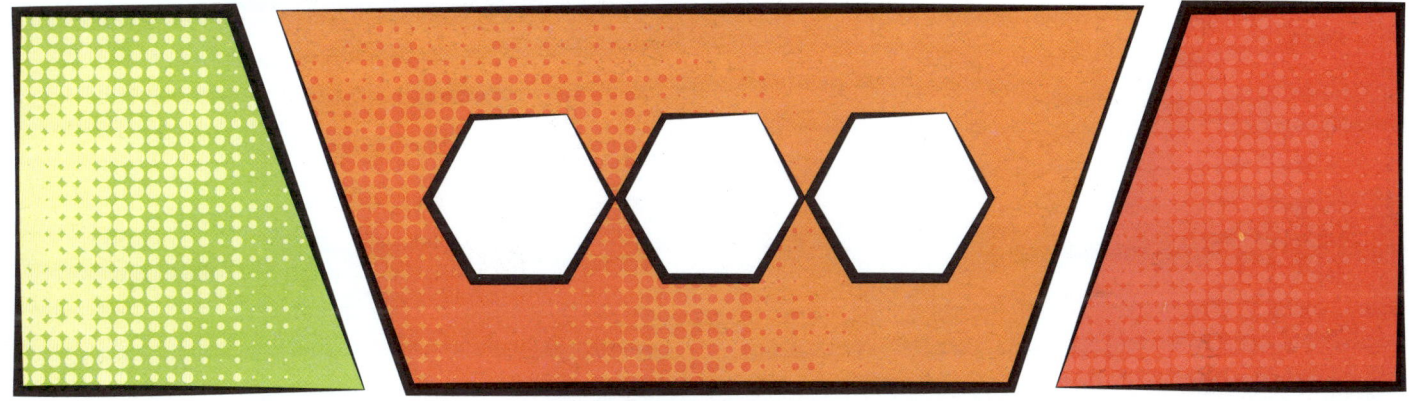

BONUS WORDS:

TIME TAKEN :

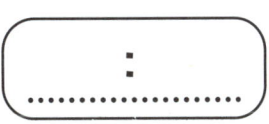

TO, TWO, SOW

9

WORD BUILDER

MAKE AS MANY WORDS AS YOU CAN WITH THE GIVEN LETTERS.

BONUS WORDS:

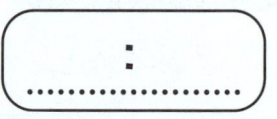

TIME TAKEN :

:
....

AT, RAT, PAR

10

WORD BUILDER

USE THE LETTERS TO FORM MEANINGFUL WORDS.

BONUS WORDS:

....

....

....

....

TIME TAKEN :

:
....

AT, TAB, BAT

WORD BUILDER

CREATE WORDS WITH THE GIVEN SET OF LETTERS.

BONUS WORDS:

TIME TAKEN :

TO, TOP, POT

12

WORD BUILDER

MAKE MEANINGFUL WORDS WITH THE GIVEN LETTERS.

BONUS WORDS:

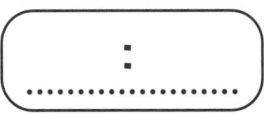

TIME TAKEN :

AN, NAB, BAN

13

WORD BUILDER

CREATE WORDS WITH THE GIVEN SET OF LETTERS.

BONUS WORDS:

TIME TAKEN :

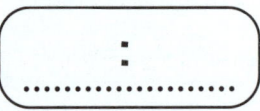

IN, BIN, NOB

14

WORD BUILDER

MAKE MEANINGFUL WORDS WITH THE GIVEN LETTERS.

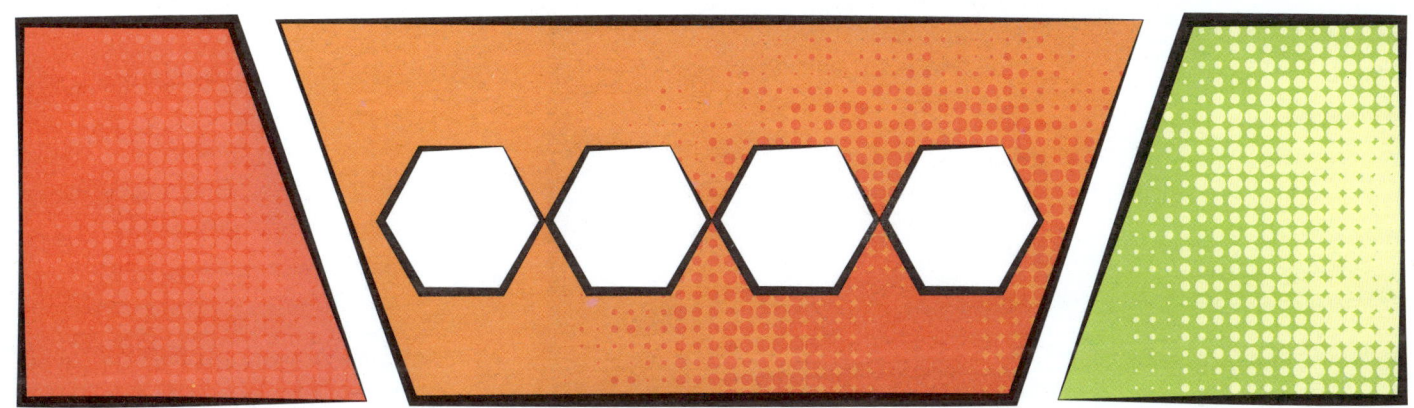

BONUS WORDS:

....
....
....
....

TIME TAKEN :

.... : ....

IT, TIC, CITY

15

WORD BUILDER

MAKE AS MANY WORDS AS YOU CAN WITH THE GIVEN LETTERS.

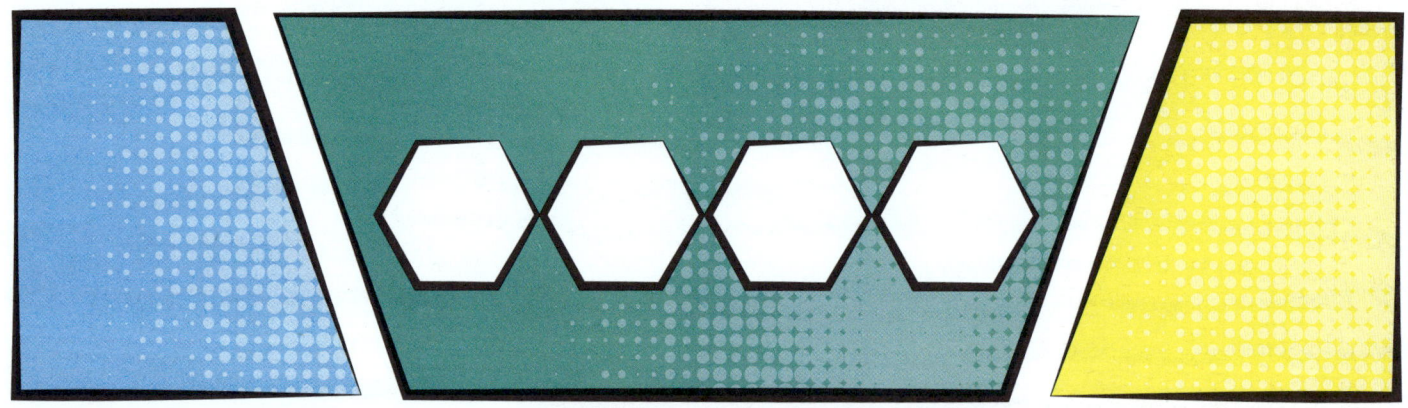

BONUS WORDS:

TIME TAKEN :

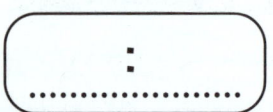

APE, GAP, PAGE

16

WORD BUILDER

USE THE LETTERS TO FORM MEANINGFUL WORDS.

BONUS WORDS:

....

....

....

....

TIME TAKEN :

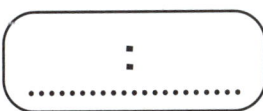

OR, TO, SO, ROT

17

CREATE WORDS WITH THE GIVEN SET OF LETTERS.

BONUS WORDS:

....

....

....

....

A T N S

TIME TAKEN :

...........:............

18

AN, AT, TAN, SAT

WORD BUILDER

MAKE MEANINGFUL WORDS WITH THE GIVEN LETTERS.

BONUS WORDS:

TIME TAKEN :

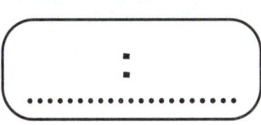

DO, TO, DOT, TAD

19

WORD BUILDER

CREATE WORDS WITH THE GIVEN SET OF LETTERS.

BONUS WORDS:

....
....
....
....

TIME TAKEN :

:
....

AM, MY, MAN, MAY

20

WORD BUILDER

MAKE MEANINGFUL WORDS WITH THE GIVEN LETTERS.

BONUS WORDS:

....

....

....

....

TIME TAKEN :

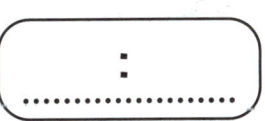

:

AS, IS, SAD, AID

21

WORD BUILDER

☆☆☆☆☆

MAKE AS MANY WORDS AS YOU CAN WITH THE GIVEN LETTERS.

BONUS WORDS:

A S

N D

TIME TAKEN :

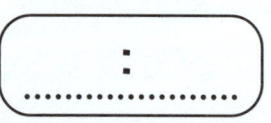

AS, AN, SAD, SAND

22

WORD BUILDER

USE THE LETTERS TO FORM MEANINGFUL WORDS.

BONUS WORDS:

....

....

....

....

TIME TAKEN :

____ : ____

IT, IN, TIN, TINY

23

WORD BUILDER

CREATE WORDS WITH THE GIVEN SET OF LETTERS.

BONUS WORDS:

TIME TAKEN :

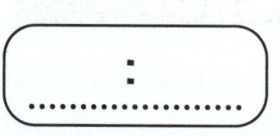

GO, GOD, DOG, GOOD

24

WORD BUILDER

MAKE MEANINGFUL WORDS WITH THE GIVEN LETTERS.

BONUS WORDS:

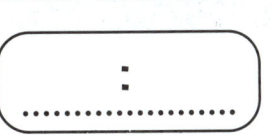

TIME TAKEN :

AT, TAP, PAT, APT

25

WORD BUILDER

CREATE WORDS WITH THE GIVEN SET OF LETTERS.

BONUS WORDS:

TIME TAKEN :

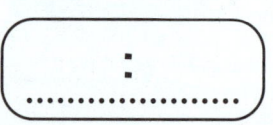

ON, WON, NOW, ONE

26

WORD BUILDER

☆☆☆☆☆

MAKE MEANINGFUL WORDS WITH THE GIVEN LETTERS.

BONUS WORDS:

....
....
....
....

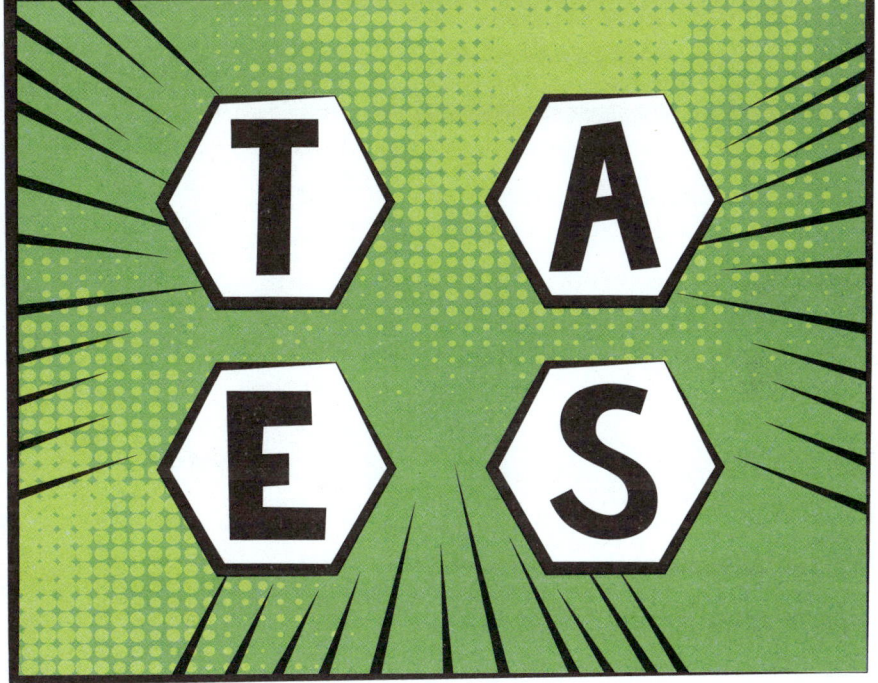

TIME TAKEN :

:
....

AT, ATE, EAT, TEA

27

WORD BUILDER

MAKE AS MANY WORDS AS YOU CAN WITH THE GIVEN LETTERS.

BONUS WORDS:

TIME TAKEN :

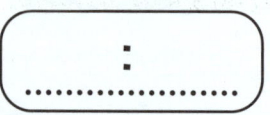

ON, NO, TON, ONE

WORD BUILDER

USE THE LETTERS TO FORM MEANINGFUL WORDS.

BONUS WORDS:

TIME TAKEN :

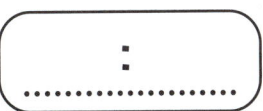

IS, ITS, SIT, TIE

WORD BUILDER

CREATE WORDS WITH THE GIVEN SET OF LETTERS.

BONUS WORDS:

TIME TAKEN :

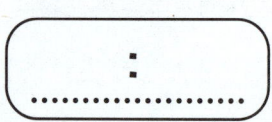

AT, TAR, RAT, EAT

WORD BUILDER

MAKE MEANINGFUL WORDS WITH THE GIVEN LETTERS.

BONUS WORDS:

TIME TAKEN :

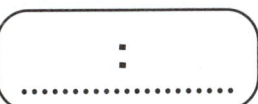

AN, BAD, AND, BAND.

31

WORD BUILDER

CREATE WORDS WITH THE GIVEN SET OF LETTERS.

BONUS WORDS:

TIME TAKEN :

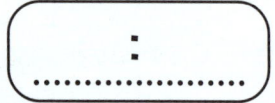

AT, SAT, SAY, STAY

32

WORD BUILDER

MAKE MEANINGFUL WORDS WITH THE GIVEN LETTERS.

BONUS WORDS:

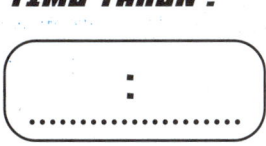

TIME TAKEN :

:

AN, PAN, LAP, PLAN

33

WORD BUILDER

MAKE AS MANY WORDS AS YOU CAN WITH THE GIVEN LETTERS.

BONUS WORDS:

TIME TAKEN :

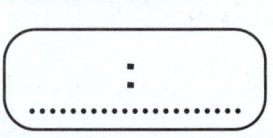

AM, RAW, WAR, WARM

WORD BUILDER

USE THE LETTERS TO FORM MEANINGFUL WORDS.

BONUS WORDS:

....
....
....
....

TIME TAKEN :

.... : ....

AS, SAY, YES, EASY

WORD BUILDER

CREATE WORDS WITH THE GIVEN SET OF LETTERS.

BONUS WORDS:

....

....

....

....

TIME TAKEN :

:
....

36

NO, TO, NOT, KNOT

WORD BUILDER

MAKE MEANINGFUL WORDS WITH THE GIVEN LETTERS.

BONUS WORDS:

....
....
....
....

TIME TAKEN :

.... : ....

AT, ATE, EAT, DATE

37

WORD BUILDER

CREATE WORDS WITH THE GIVEN SET OF LETTERS.

BONUS WORDS:

....

....

....

....

TIME TAKEN :

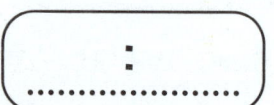

: ....

DO, LOG, OLD, GOLD

38

WORD BUILDER

MAKE MEANINGFUL WORDS WITH THE GIVEN LETTERS.

BONUS WORDS:

....

....

....

....

TIME TAKEN :

:

....

WE, WIN, NEW, WINE

WORD BUILDER

MAKE AS MANY WORDS AS YOU CAN WITH THE GIVEN LETTERS.

BONUS WORDS:

TIME TAKEN :

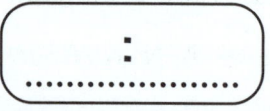

40

IN, NT, TIN, MINT

WORD BUILDER

USE THE LETTERS TO FORM MEANINGFUL WORDS.

BONUS WORDS:

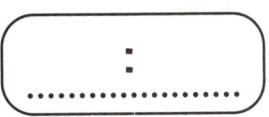

TIME TAKEN :

.... : ....

OR, ORB, BOA, BOAR

41

WORD BUILDER

CREATE WORDS WITH THE GIVEN SET OF LETTERS.

BONUS WORDS:

G A N E L

TIME TAKEN :

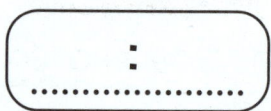

42

AN, LEG, NAG, LEAN

WORD BUILDER

MAKE MEANINGFUL WORDS WITH THE GIVEN LETTERS.

BONUS WORDS:

TIME TAKEN :

IT, TEN, HIT, THEN

43

WORD BUILDER

CREATE WORDS WITH THE GIVEN SET OF LETTERS.

BONUS WORDS:

....

....

....

....

TIME TAKEN :

.........:.........

TO, NOT, TON, TORN

44

WORD BUILDER

MAKE MEANINGFUL WORDS WITH THE GIVEN LETTERS.

BONUS WORDS:

....

....

....

....

R E E A S

TIME TAKEN :

:

....

AS, ARE, SEA, EASE

45

WORD BUILDER

MAKE AS MANY WORDS AS YOU CAN WITH THE GIVEN LETTERS.

BONUS WORDS:

....

....

....

....

TIME TAKEN :

.... :

TO, TOE, MET, TOTE

46

WORD BUILDER

USE THE LETTERS TO FORM MEANINGFUL WORDS.

BONUS WORDS:

....

....

....

....

TIME TAKEN :

ON, SON, LAN, LOAN

47

WORD BUILDER

CREATE WORDS WITH THE GIVEN SET OF LETTERS.

BONUS WORDS:

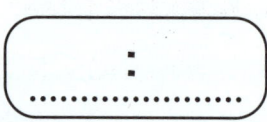

SO, NOR, SOW, SNOW

TIME TAKEN :

48

WORD BUILDER

MAKE MEANINGFUL WORDS WITH THE GIVEN LETTERS.

BONUS WORDS:

....

....

....

....

TIME TAKEN :

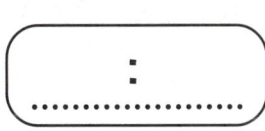

:

....

AS, ASH, FAT, FAST

WORD BUILDER

CREATE WORDS WITH THE GIVEN SET OF LETTERS.

BONUS WORDS:

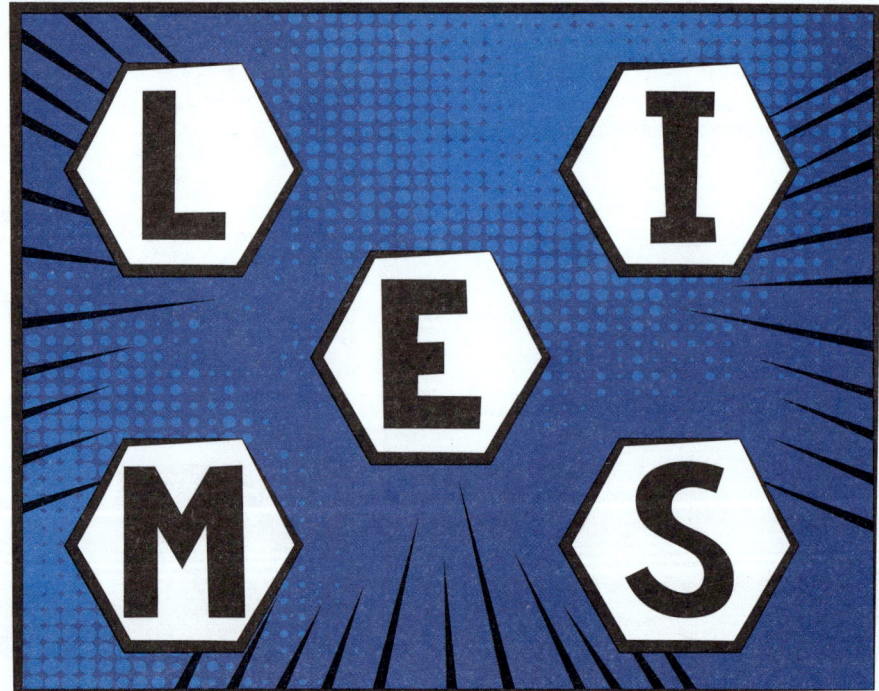

TIME TAKEN :

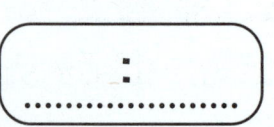

IS, LIE, SIE, SLIM

50

WORD BUILDER

MAKE MEANINGFUL WORDS WITH THE GIVEN LETTERS.

BONUS WORDS:

TIME TAKEN :

:

IT, SIT, WIT, STIR

WORD BUILDER

MAKE AS MANY WORDS AS YOU CAN WITH THE GIVEN LETTERS.

BONUS WORDS:

SEE, LET, EEL, LETS

WORD BUILDER

USE THE LETTERS TO FORM MEANINGFUL WORDS.

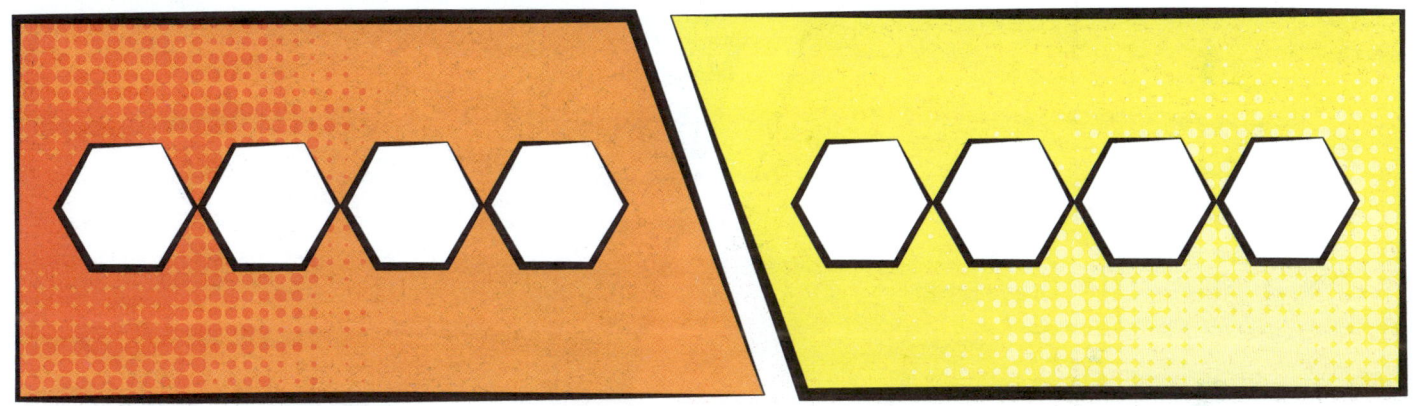

BONUS WORDS:

TIME TAKEN :

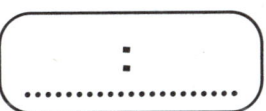

AN, PEN, LANE, PANE

53

WORD BUILDER

CREATE WORDS WITH THE GIVEN SET OF LETTERS.

BONUS WORDS:

TIME TAKEN :

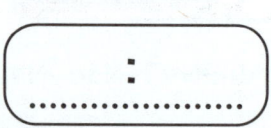

ME, MAN, MANE, MEAN

54

WORD BUILDER

MAKE MEANINGFUL WORDS WITH THE GIVEN LETTERS.

BONUS WORDS:

....

....

....

....

TIME TAKEN :

.... : ....

IS, SIN, SIGN, SING

55

WORD BUILDER

CREATE WORDS WITH THE GIVEN SET OF LETTERS.

BONUS WORDS:

AS, SAT, SALT, LAST

WORD BUILDER

MAKE MEANINGFUL WORDS WITH THE GIVEN LETTERS.

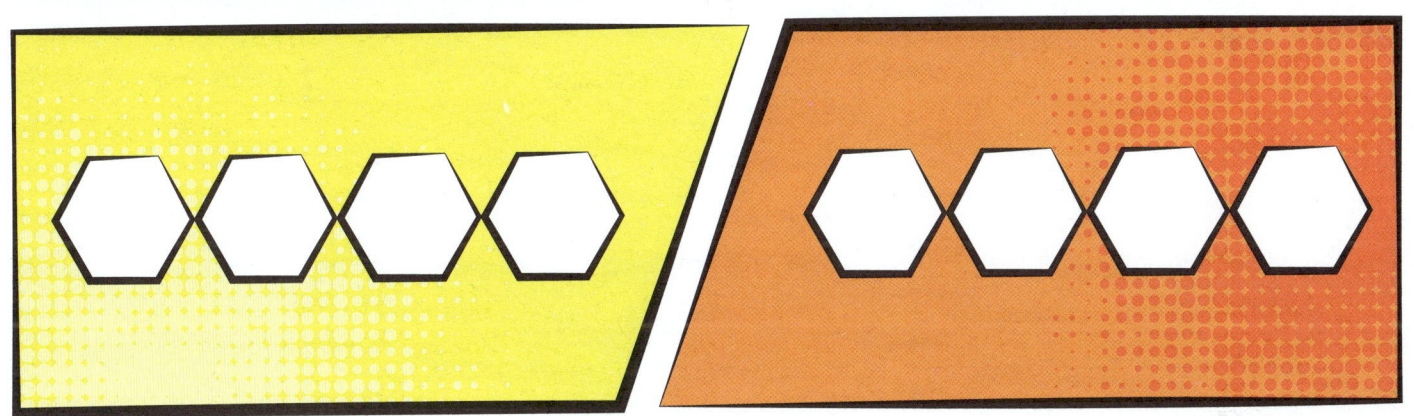

BONUS WORDS:

....

....

....

....

TIME TAKEN :

:
....

57

WORD BUILDER

MAKE AS MANY WORDS AS YOU CAN WITH THE GIVEN LETTERS.

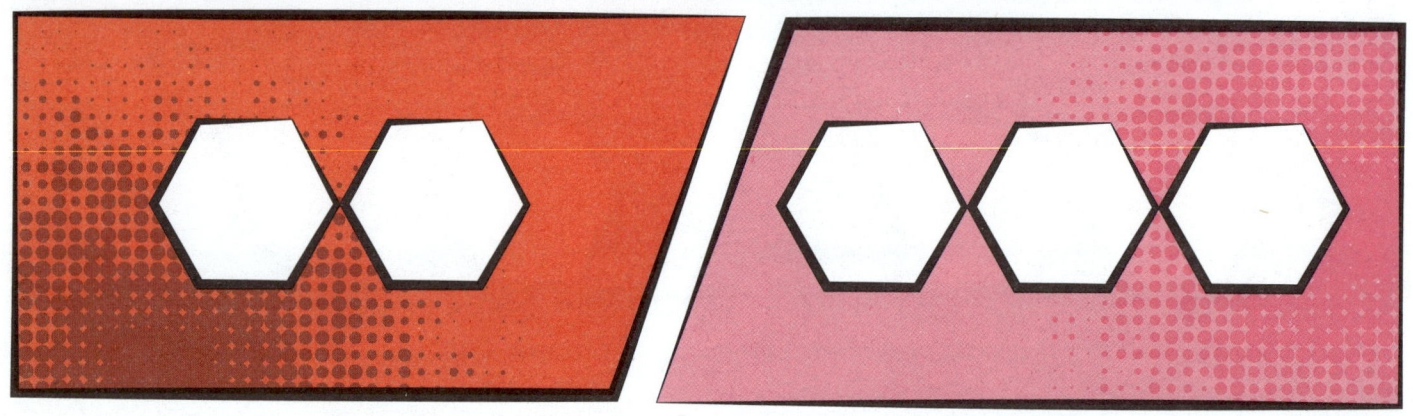

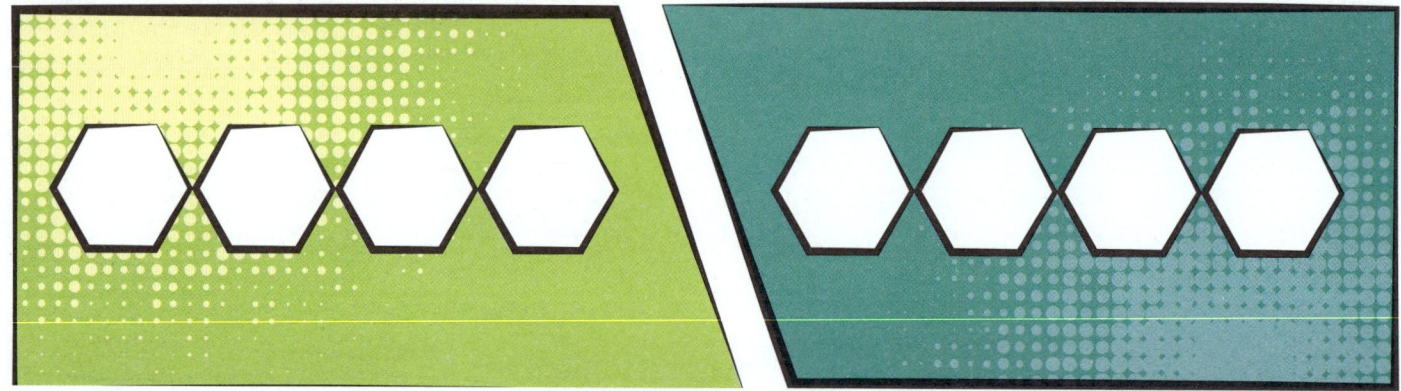

BONUS WORDS:

....

....

....

....

TIME TAKEN :

.... :

AM, CAM, CALM, CLAM

58

WORD BUILDER

USE THE LETTERS TO FORM MEANINGFUL WORDS.

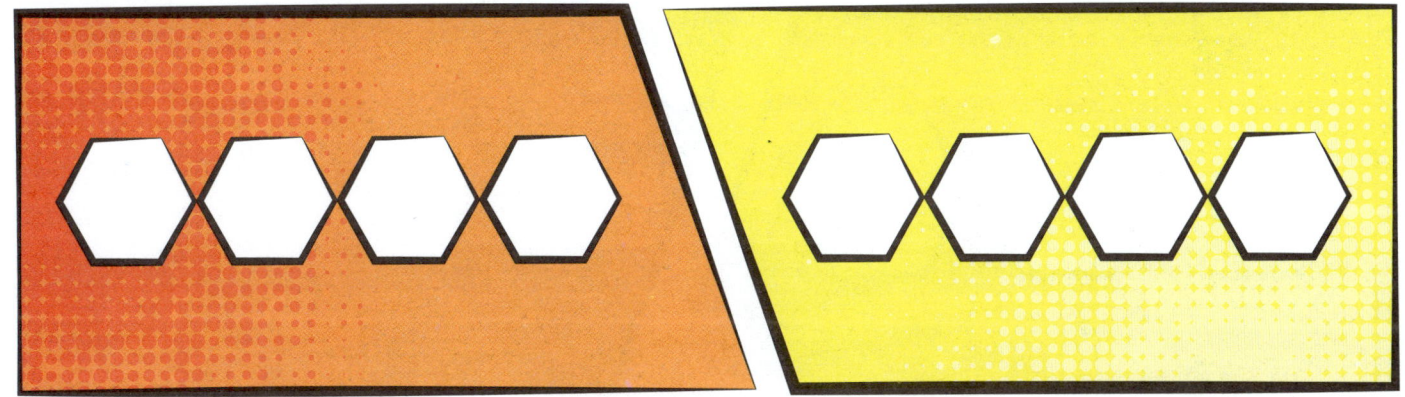

BONUS WORDS:

E S R U

TIME TAKEN :

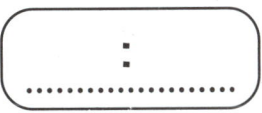

US, USE, SURE, USER

WORD BUILDER

CREATE WORDS WITH THE GIVEN SET OF LETTERS.

BONUS WORDS:

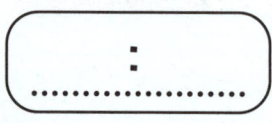

TIME TAKEN :

AT, TAN, NUT, AUNT

WORD BUILDER

MAKE MEANINGFUL WORDS WITH THE GIVEN LETTERS.

BONUS WORDS:

TIME TAKEN :

:
....

TO, COT, SCOT, TOSS

61

WORD BUILDER

CREATE WORDS WITH THE GIVEN SET OF LETTERS.

BONUS WORDS:

TIME TAKEN :

HE, HER, HERE, TREE

62

WORD BUILDER

MAKE MEANINGFUL WORDS WITH THE GIVEN LETTERS.

BONUS WORDS:

....

....

....

....

TIME TAKEN :

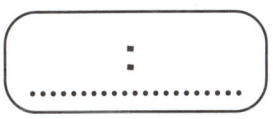

:

....

OR, ORB, BORN, IRON

63

WORD BUILDER

MAKE AS MANY WORDS AS YOU CAN WITH THE GIVEN LETTERS.

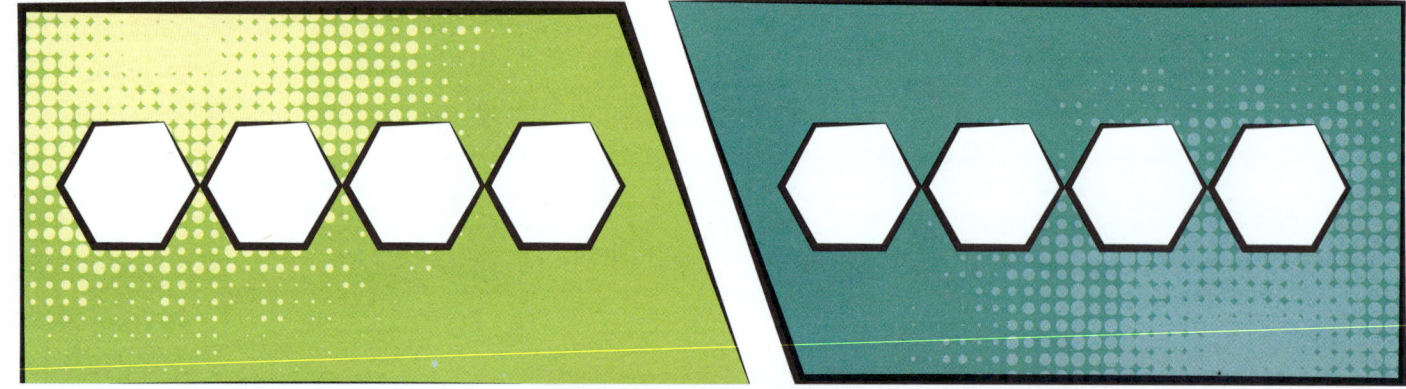

BONUS WORDS:

....

....

....

....

TIME TAKEN :

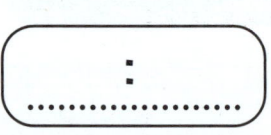

HE, ASH, SEAL, LASH